QUITTING
IS NOT AN
OPTION

First published by LAUREN MOOI Publishing

Copyright © 2025 by Dr. R. van Reenen

All rights reserved. No part of this publication may be reproduced, stored, or transmitted in any form or by any means, electronic, mechanical, photocopying, recording, scanning, or otherwise, without written permission from the author. It is illegal to copy this book, post it to a website, or distribute it by any other means without permission.

Dr. R. van Reenen asserts the moral right to be identified as the author of this work under the Copyright Act 98 of 1978

First Edition June 2025, paperback and eBook

ISBN: 978-1-0370-8390-7

www.laurenmooipublishing.com

Dedication

To the weary warrior,

Who stood when others sat. Who cried in silence and prayed in faith. Who almost gave up but didn't. This book is for you. And to my Savior, Jesus Christ, who never quits on us. May this work glorify You and encourage those still running their race.

Preface

In every generation, there rises a call; a deep, resounding echo in the soul of humanity that challenges the status quo, confronts adversity, and insists on perseverance against all odds. *"Quitting Is Not an Option"* is the call for this generation.

Dr. R. van Reenen has lived through seasons of challenge, transition, and growth, not only in his personal journey but also in his leadership across the spheres of faith, education, and economic thought. This book is not simply a collection of motivational clichés; it is a battle-tested manual for those who feel the weight of giving up pressing down on them. The message is urgent. The world needs leaders, dreamers, parents, entrepreneurs, pastors, and young people who will stand when all else tells them to sit down. We need voices that rise above the noise of defeat and declare with conviction, "I will not quit!"

Introduction

There are moments in life that define us. Not the victories, not even the accolades, but the decision not to quit when it would have been easier to walk away. I have faced those moments. Perhaps you have, too. Quitting Is Not an Option was born out of these defining moments. As a leader, father, scholar, and pastor, I have experienced the highs of success and the depths of discouragement. But in each valley, I found that God's strength is made perfect in our weakness, not through the avoidance of struggle, but in the refusal to surrender to it. This book is not a lecture but a conversation between fellow travellers. Whether you are standing at the edge of burnout, battling inner turmoil, recovering from failure, or building a dream from the ground up, this book is for you. We will explore stories, both biblical and modern, that remind us that the greats were never those who had it easy, but those who chose to stay in the race. We will dive into practical strategies to reignite purpose, refocus vision, and restructure failure into fuel. We will confront spiritual weariness, financial breakdown, relational pain, and leadership fatigue and emerge stronger. I invite you to journey through these chapters with an open heart and a fighting spirit. The world is waiting for your yes, your persistence, your voice, and your breakthrough. Because quitting? It is not an option.

Instructions

Dear Reader,

Welcome to Quitting Is Not an Option. This book was written with you in mind. Yes, you who have wrestled with disappointment, faced overwhelming odds, and perhaps even entertained the thought of giving up. Whether you are a leader, a student, a parent, a pastor, or a seeker of purpose, this book serves as a companion for your journey through pain, perseverance, and personal growth.

As you read through each chapter, here are a few guidelines to help you get the most from this book:

1. **Read Slowly and Reflectively**
    Don't rush through the pages. Each chapter is intentionally layered with biblical truths, real-life stories, and insights to guide your heart and mind. Pause when something resonates; highlight, underline, or journal your thoughts.

2. **Engage with the Scriptures**
    You will find biblical references throughout the book. Take the time to read these passages in your Bible. Allow God's Word to shape your perspective and renew your strength.

3. **Apply the Lessons Personally**

Every chapter concludes with key reflections or takeaways. Reflect on how these principles relate to your life, challenges, and calling. Allow the lessons to resonate deeply. Utilize this book daily as a spiritual booster to align your focus, build endurance, and reignite your faith.

4. **Share and Discuss**
   If this book resonates with you, don't keep it to yourself. Share it with a friend, your church group, or anyone you know who is on the brink of quitting. It may just be the lifeline they need.

5. **Keep Going**
   Above all, this book is a call to action: to rise, endure, and press on. Remember that your pain has a purpose, no matter how heavy the burden or how long the journey is. Your race is not over; quitting is not an option.

May the words on these pages awaken courage, renew your vision, and rekindle your hope.

With purpose and passion,
Dr. R. van Reenen

Chapter 1
When You Feel Like Giving Up

There's a moment, quiet, heavy, and often hidden from the public eye, when the thought of quitting creeps in. It might come after another failed attempt, rejection letter, or silent prayer with no answer. The weight becomes unbearable, and the question arises: "Is it really worth it?"

If you've ever asked that question, you are not alone. Even the strongest among us reach the brink of surrender.

The Secret Battle

Most people don't see the internal battles of those who seem to have it all together. They observe the polished presentations, the Sunday sermons, the business suits, and the smiling family portraits; however, behind the scenes lies a war zone of emotions, fatigue, doubt, and

QUITTING
IS NOT AN
OPTION

By

Dr. R. van Reenen

Table of Contents

Dedication 2
Preface 3
Introduction 4
Instructions 5
Chapter 1: When You Feel Like Giving Up 7
Chapter 2: Embracing the Pain Without Losing the Purpose .. 22
Chapter 3: The Power of a Made-Up Mind 37
Chapter 4: Storm-Proof Vision 51
Chapter 5: Carrying the Cross, The Cost of Commitment 66
Chapter 6: Burned but not Broken 81
Chapter 7: Grace for the Grit 97
Chapter 8: The Silence Between Seasons 112
Chapter 9: When the Finish Line Moves 126
Chapter 10: Quitting is Not an Option 140
Appendix: Tools for the Journey 155
About the Author 159
Acknowledgements 161

discouragement. For years, I've ministered to leaders who stood in pulpits yet were silently planning their exit. I've spoken with parents who are ready to walk away from children they love but no longer understand. I've counselled entrepreneurs who invested their last cent into a dream, still struggling to break even. The truth is, the thought of quitting is more common than we admit. But just because it visits, doesn't mean it has to stay.

Biblical Perspective: Elijah Under the Tree

One of the most powerful stories of burnout and near-quitting is found in 1 Kings 19. Elijah, the mighty prophet of fire, had just faced the prophets of Baal in a miraculous showdown. Fire fell from heaven. A national revival was on the brink. Yet, one chapter later, we find him alone in the wilderness, under a broom tree, praying to die.
"I have had enough, Lord," he said. "Take my life..." (1 Kings 19:4 NIV). How can a man so anointed, powerful, and victorious end up in that place? Because even the strongest feel like quitting. But God did not rebuke Elijah; He gave him rest. He sent an angel. He offered food, companionship, and eventually a fresh commission. Elijah wasn't done. And neither are you.

Practical Reflection:
Recognize the Warning Signs

Before quitting turns into action, it starts as exhaustion. Here are several signs that you are approaching the edge:

1. **Loss of Motivation:** The tasks you once loved now feel burdensome.
2. **Emotional Numbness:** You're no longer deeply sad but simply empty.
3. **Isolation:** You withdraw from others and sink into silence.
4. **Negative Self-Talk:** "I'm a failure," "This will never work," "Why bother?"
5. **Fantasy of Escape:** You dream of simply walking away.

These are not signs of weakness; instead, they are signals that something requires attention. Instead of giving up, we must lean in with grace and strategy.

Leadership Insight:
Quitting isn't just personal, it's communal

When a leader quits, a ripple effect follows. Whether you're a pastor, manager, parent, or peer, your perseverance, or lack thereof, affects others. Imagine Moses, standing before the Red Sea with a terrified nation behind him. The pressure was immense, the people complained, and the odds were against him. But Moses didn't quit. He raised his staff, and God moved. Your courage to continue may be the turning point for someone else's miracle.

What to Do When You Feel Like Quitting

1. **Rest Before You Resign:** Fatigue often clouds judgment. Step away, if necessary, but don't decide while depleted.
2. **Speak to Someone Safe:** You don't need thousands, just one or two trusted voices to remind you of who you are.
3. **Revisit Your 'Why':** Reflect on the original vision. What motivated your start? What problem did you aim to solve? What dream were you pursuing?
4. **Pray and Listen:** God's silence is sometimes an invitation to intimacy, not abandonment. His stillness is not absence.
5. **Recalibrate, Don't Abort:** Adjust the sails, but don't abandon the ship. Sometimes the mission is correct, but the method needs adjusting.

A Word for You

If you're reading this and feel like you've lost your fire, I want to speak life into your soul. You are not a failure. You are not forgotten. You are not disqualified. Your value does not decrease because of fatigue. Your calling is not nullified by a season of doubt. What you carry is still needed. And what's ahead of you is greater than what's behind you. The enemy would love nothing more than to convince you to give up. If you quit, generations might never see what God planted in you. This book is titled "Quitting Is Not an Option" for a reason. You were made for more. And we're just getting started.

Journal notes

Chapter 2
Embracing the Pain Without Losing the Purpose

Pain and purpose often ride in the same chariot. We tend to believe that if something hurts, it must not be right, and that difficulty means we've taken the wrong turn. But what if pain is not an indicator of misdirection, but rather a signal that you are on the path of transformation? This chapter explores how we can endure pain without letting it destroy our purpose and how some of the most significant breakthroughs are born out of our darkest valleys.

The Purpose in the Pain

Pain has a voice. It speaks in the night, interrupts your day, and lingers in silence. But pain is also a revealer. It tells you what matters most. It shows you what's broken. It unveils what you've tried to bury. Many people try to avoid pain at all costs. They change jobs, churches, relationships, and locations, all in an attempt to escape discomfort. However, you cannot outrun internal pain with external changes.

"He was despised and rejected… a man of sorrows, and familiar with suffering." (Isaiah 53:3 NIV). Jesus Himself was not exempt from pain; yet, through His suffering, the greatest redemption in history was made available. There is power in walking through pain with purpose.

Joseph: From the Pit to the Palace

Joseph's life is a vivid example. Betrayed by his brothers, sold into slavery, falsely accused, and unjustly imprisoned, his story reads like a tragedy. Yet, each chapter of pain was a step closer to his destiny. What would have happened if Joseph had given up in prison? He would have never become the second most powerful man in Egypt. He would've missed the reunion with his family. He would've forfeited the role of saviour to a starving nation. His pain didn't cancel his purpose; it prepared him for it.

The Three Lies Pain Tells You

1. **"This will never end."** Pain tries to convince you it's permanent. But seasons change. What feels like forever today can turn into a memory tomorrow.

2. **"You're the only one going through this."** Pain isolates. It makes you feel like you're uniquely broken. However, others have travelled similar paths and survived.
3. **"You must have done something wrong."** Pain masquerades as punishment. However, not all suffering results from sin. Sometimes, it's an indicator of growth.

Turning Pain into Fuel

You have two options with pain: you can allow it to define you, or you can allow it to refine you.

A. Journal the Journey
Write it down. Every lesson. Every tear. Every moment of clarity. Someday, your journal will become someone else's survival guide.

B. Serve Through the Suffering
Find someone else to encourage. Pour into others while you are healing. This isn't hypocrisy; it's leadership. Even in your brokenness, you embody healing.

C. Let God Reframe the Narrative
Instead of asking, "Why me?", ask, "What now?" God never wastes pain. He will use what the enemy meant for evil for good if we stay the course.

Leadership Insight: Pain builds authority

Genuine authority is built not in comfort but through hardship. Leaders who have experienced pain, shed tears, and struggled to triumph are the voices that command trust. After enduring trials, your voice carries a profound resonance. There's no need to pretend to be strong when you have weathered the storm. When you serve, speak, lead, write, or provide counsel from a place of healed pain, people not only hear your words; they truly feel them.

When You Feel Like You Can't Take Another Step

Take it anyway. If you need to cry, cry. If you need to scream, scream. If you need to crawl, crawl. But don't stop. Don't give in. Don't give up. Your pain is not your final chapter.

You are Still in the Story

Let me tell you something: the fact that you're reading this book means you still believe there's more. Deep down, beyond the tears and trauma, your soul is crying out for life. This chapter serves as your permission slip to stop hiding your pain and start transforming it. Not by denying it, but by facing it and walking through it with courage.

Quitting is not an option because your purpose is still present, even in the pain.

Journal notes

Chapter 3
The Power of a Made-Up Mind

There's nothing more unstoppable than a determined mind. Talent can be wasted, resources can dwindle, and circumstances can change, but a mind that is resolutely decided will find a way where there seems to be none. Choosing not to quit is more than a feeling; it is a spiritual discipline. It's the setting of your internal compass, regardless of the external storm.

The Battle is in the Mind

Long before defeat occurs in reality, it first takes place in the mind. The thoughts you entertain become the beliefs you live by. That's why discouragement is such a dangerous enemy: not because it alters your situation, but because it changes your perception of it.
"As a man thinketh in his heart, so is he." (Proverbs 23:7 NIV). You can have an open door in front of you and still miss it because your mindset is trapped in fear.

Conversely, you can be locked in a prison and still walk in freedom if your mind is made up.

Jesus in Gethsemane: The power of surrendered resolve

In the garden of Gethsemane, Jesus experienced a moment of agony so intense that He sweated blood. The pain of what was coming was overwhelming. But then He said, "*Nevertheless, not my will, but Yours be done*" (Luke 22:42 NIV). That was the moment of resolve. The cross didn't kill Jesus; His surrender did. He had already died in His will before He was nailed to the wood. That's the power of a made-up mind. The battle was won before the first whip ever touched His back.

Make Up Your Mind Before the Storm Hits

You can't wait until you're under attack to decide whether to fight; you must choose now.

Make up your mind:

- That you will finish.
- That you will forgive.
- That you will not go back.
- That you will rise again.

When the storm arrives, you won't need to decide; you'll simply carry out what you have already determined in your spirit.

Keys to a Resolute Mindset

1. Speak Life Over Yourself

Your voice is the first that your spirit hears each morning. Stop waiting for others to encourage you; speak your victory out loud.
"I will not die here."
"This is not the end of me."
"God's purpose for my life will not be aborted."

2. Remove the Exit Option

Burn the escape plan. If you always keep a door open to quitting, you'll eventually use it.
Commit to the calling even when it's inconvenient. Burn the boats like the old explorers did, no retreat, no return.

3. Feed Your Focus

What you focus on multiplies. Nourish your faith by reading, praying, journaling, and surrounding yourself with committed people.

4. Practice Mental Rehearsal

Athletes visualize success before experiencing it. Leaders should do the same. Rehearse the win in your mind. Speak it. See it. Walk as if it's already done.

What Happens when You Decide to Finish?

The atmosphere shifts when resolve enters the room. Heaven supports a determined mind. Your decision invites divine help. "But Daniel purposed in his heart…" (Daniel 1:8 NIV). Before Daniel ever saw God shut the lions' mouths or deliver him from the fiery furnace, he resolved in his heart not to compromise. That decision granted him supernatural favour and unshakable peace.

Make the Decision Today

Right now, decide that you will not quit. Believe that your marriage will thrive. Trust that your ministry will finish strong. Know that your health, career, and family will rise again. You don't need everything to be perfect; you need to decide. Once your mind is made up, your enemy has lost his advantage.

Journal notes

Chapter 4
Storm-Proof Vision

Vision is the anchor of endurance. When life turns dark and the waves rise, vision keeps you from drifting. However, not every vision can survive a storm. What you need is storm-proof vision. Vision that is strong enough to endure trials, flexible enough to adjust with time, and deep enough to keep you grounded in purpose. Storm-proof vision is not just a good idea; it's a lifeline.

What is Vision, really?

Vision is not a five-year plan or a mission statement on the wall. Vision is a deeply rooted sense of purpose, identity, and direction. It drives your decisions and defines your legacy. "Where there is no vision, the people perish." (Proverbs 29:18 NIV). Without vision, we become reactive, tossed by every wave of circumstance. With vision, we become proactive, walking by faith rather than by sight.

The Nature of Storms

Storms don't ask for permission. They arrive uninvited, often disrupting progress. A storm can be:

- A diagnosis
- A betrayal
- A financial crash
- A moral failure
- A loss you didn't see coming

In these moments, the real question arises: *Can your vision outlast the weather?*

Biblical Anchor: Paul in the storm

In Acts 27, Paul finds himself on a ship in the middle of a violent storm. The crew panics as the ship begins to break apart, and supplies are thrown overboard. Hope starts to fade. Yet, Paul stands amid the chaos and declares: "But now I urge you to keep up your courage, because not one of you will be lost... Last night an angel of the God to whom I belong and whom I serve stood beside me." (Acts 27:22-23 NIV). Paul received a vision from God. He knew he wasn't going to die in that storm because his assignment wasn't over. His vision gave him courage, not just for himself, but for everyone on board.

Signs of Storm-Proof Vision

1. It Doesn't Depend on Applause

Storm-proof vision doesn't die when people stop clapping. If your purpose requires constant validation, it's not vision; it's vanity.

2. It Grows Stronger in Isolation

Some of your clearest moments will come in lonely seasons. Storm-proof vision hears God more clearly in the silence.

3. It Survives Closed Doors

When one door closes, storm-proof vision persists; it knocks again or builds a new door.

4. It Endures Delayed Results

Storm-proof vision isn't dissuaded by slow progress. It recognises that growth is often invisible before it becomes undeniable.

Developing Storm-Proof Vision

1. Clarify the Core

What has God called you to do, build, protect, or leave behind? Clarify your why. If your vision is unclear, your endurance will waver.

2. Write it Down

"Write the vision and make it plain." (Habakkuk 2:2 NIV). Capture your vision in writing so you can revisit it when the winds howl. When emotions cloud your mind, your written vision will serve as a reminder for your soul.

3. Return to the Source

Never allow your vision to outrun your prayer life. Return to the One who bestowed upon you the dream. Ask Him to strengthen and refine it as you grow.

4. Share it with the Right People

Storm-proof vision must be nurtured. Share it with people who will hold you accountable and pray it into reality alongside you, not with individuals who will poke holes in it.

Leadership Insight: Vision protects the people you lead

As a leader, your clarity brings safety to others. If you falter in a crisis, those you lead will scatter. However, when your vision remains clear, even when everything else is shaking, it becomes a lighthouse in the storm. Storm-proof vision doesn't just keep you safe; it offers shelter to those around you.

A Word for Visionaries Who Feel Weary

You might feel that your vision is too big, too slow, or too misunderstood. But don't let temporary storms deter you from eternal assignments. If God gave you the vision, He also provided the grace to endure the storm. Hold fast, stay the course, and keep your eyes focused not on the clouds, but on the promise. Your vision is still alive, and it is strong enough to survive this.

Journal notes

Chapter 5
Carrying the Cross
The Cost of Commitment

Commitment is not glamorous. It is not loud. It does not always come with applause. But it is the thread that connects calling to completion. To commit is to choose the difficult road, not just once, but repeatedly. Carrying the cross illustrates this type of commitment. Not a decorative, gold-plated cross, but the real one. The one that bruises your shoulder, bleeds on your back, and reminds you: purpose comes with a price.

The Call to Carry

"If anyone desires to come after Me, let him deny himself, take up his cross daily, and follow Me." (Luke 9:23 NIV). Jesus did not promise ease. He promised meaning. To follow Him is to carry the cross of commitment through hardship, ridicule, loneliness, and pressure.

Commitment means staying when it would be easier to walk away. It means choosing sacrifice over comfort, integrity over popularity, and legacy over luxury.

The Myth of Easy Obedience

There is a lie that says, "If it's from God, it will be easy." No. If it's from God, it will stretch you. It will break you in the best way. It will expose your selfishness and call you into deeper surrender. Every person in Scripture who accomplished something great had to carry a cross of commitment:

- **Abraham** had to leave everything familiar.
- **Ruth** had to follow Naomi into a foreign land.
- **David** was anointed but not yet appointed for years.
- **Esther** risked her life to speak truth to power.

Each story includes pain. Delay. Conflict. And yet, not one of them quit.

What Commitment Really Costs

1. **Comfort**
   Commitment requires you to do things that inconvenience your flesh. Early mornings, late

nights, missed opportunities, and difficult conversations are all part of the price.

2. **Control**
   You must let go of your expectations for how things will unfold. Genuine commitment lies not in your plan, but in God's process.

3. **Approval**
   People may not always understand your dedication. They might mock your decisions or misinterpret your motives. Commitment often feels lonely.

4. **Options**
   You can't say yes to everything. Commitment requires a focused "no" to many good things to say "yes" to the right one.

The Strength Found in Surrender

Here's the paradox: the cross that feels burdensome becomes your badge of honour. The thing you thought would break you becomes the very thing that builds you. Jesus didn't endure the cross because it was easy. He did it because of the joy set before Him (Hebrews 12:2). He saw you. And that was enough. When your commitment is fuelled by love, love for God, for people, for purpose, it becomes sustainable.

Leadership Insight:
People don't follow talent, they follow tenacity

In leadership, people aren't inspired by how gifted you are; they're drawn to how committed you are. Anyone can start a project, but very few stay with it long enough to finish. Your team, family, congregation, or business doesn't just need your passion; they need your perseverance. They'll pick up theirs when they see you carry your cross without quitting.

Commitment is not about Perfection, but Persistence.

You will stumble. You will have days when quitting sounds more appealing than continuing. But don't confuse weakness with unworthiness. Keep showing up. Keep pressing on. Keep carrying your cross. And when you feel weak, remember this:
"My grace is sufficient for you, for My strength is made perfect in weakness." (2 Corinthians 12:9 NIV). You are not carrying the cross alone. Jesus carried His, so you have the strength to carry yours.

You can still Choose to Stay

You don't have to feel strong to be committed. You don't have to see the end to keep walking. You don't need applause to validate your obedience. What you need is a made-up mind, a submitted heart, and a willingness to carry what matters most. Ultimately, it's not the most talented who finishes; it's the most committed.

Journal notes

Chapter 6
Burned but not Broken

Scars tell a story. Not of weakness, but of survival. Not of defeat, but of resilience. Everyone who walks with purpose will walk through fire; if you're honest, you might be carrying the residue of battles past. Burned? Yes. But broken? Never. There is a difference between being wounded and being ruined. The fire may have touched you, but it didn't consume you. You are still here. And that is proof of purpose.

The Reality of the Fire

We all encounter seasons when everything seems to burn: our plans, our expectations, even our faith. These are moments when:

- A trusted friend betrays you.
- A business collapses.
- A marriage suffers.

- A church splits.
- A door you prayed for slams shut.

In those moments, the heat feels unbearable. But fire isn't just destructive; it's also refining. "When you walk through the fire, you shall not be burned, nor shall the flame scorch you." (Isaiah 43:2 NIV). Notice: You will walk through it, not around it. And you will come out the other side.

Biblical Example: The three Hebrew boys

In Daniel 3, Shadrach, Meshach, and Abednego refused to bow to a golden idol. Their refusal came with a price: they were thrown into a fiery furnace. But when King Nebuchadnezzar looked into the fire, he saw not three, but four, and the fourth looked like a son of the gods. (Daniel 3:25 NIV). The fire was meant to destroy them, but it only destroyed the ropes that bound them. They walked freely in what was designed to finish them. And most profoundly, they weren't alone. The presence of God showed up in the fire, not before it. This is the promise for every committed soul: **God doesn't always deliver you from the fire, but He will always meet you in it.**

What Fire Reveals

1. **Your identity:** Fire reveals whether you're building on straw or stone. When the heat intensifies, your true foundation is exposed. If your identity is rooted in Christ, you may feel the heat, but you won't crumble.
2. **Your community:** When you're on fire, people either lean in or walk out. Pain reveals your circle. Some friends are for comfort; others are for the call. Storms reveal which is which.
3. **Your calling:** Some callings are ignited by adversity. The fire that tries to end you often pushes you into your next level. Many ministries, movements, and messages are born in a blaze.

Healing from Burnout

You can be burned by people, churches, leadership roles, or family. Burnout isn't always due to doing too much; it often results from engaging in activities that aren't aligned with your grace or carrying more than you're called to.

How to Heal:
- **Rest Without Guilt:** Jesus rested. So should you. Restoration is not weakness; it's wisdom.

- **Talk About It:** Suppressed pain becomes silent poison. Share your experiences with trusted, godly counsel.
- **Rediscover Your Why:** Sometimes we forget the vision that motivated us to start. Go back to the beginning and re-anchor yourself in God's voice.
- **Let God Be Your Firefighter:** Allow Him to extinguish the embers of bitterness, offense, and unforgiveness. These are dangerous if left unchecked.

"He heals the broken-hearted and binds up their wounds." (Psalm 147:3 NIV)

You May Be Singed, But You're Still Standing

There is a reason you've survived things others couldn't. It's not luck; it's purpose. The enemy couldn't take you out because there's still too much in you to come forth. You were burned but not broken, and your scars are holy; they speak of a Savior who stood with you in the smoke.

Leadership Insight:
The most authentic leaders lead with limping feet

If you want to connect with people's hearts, don't lead from a place of perfection; lead from a place of redemption. When processed correctly, your pain becomes someone else's permission to heal.

The fire gave you:

- Compassion
- Depth
- Humility
- Authority

Your leadership is deeper because of what you've endured.

Final Encouragement

If you're walking through fire right now, don't stop. Don't sit down. Don't give in. The fire is temporary. The fruit is eternal. And when you emerge, because you *will*, you'll carry something unshakable: *the testimony of a survivor.* You are not broken. You are battle-tested. You are still breathing. And if there is breath in your lungs, there is still purpose in your life.

Journal notes

Chapter 7
Grace for the Grit

There's a point in every journey where human strength fails. Muscles ache. Motivation fades. Your feet move, but your soul is weary. And in that sacred moment, when grit is no longer enough, **grace steps in.** This is the intersection where heaven meets hustle, where supernatural help upholds your natural determination. Grit gets you started; grace gets you through.

What is Grit?

Grit is your willingness to keep showing up. It encompasses discipline, resilience, and mental toughness. Grit means getting up when no one's watching. It involves leading, loving, and labouring, even when it hurts. "Let us not grow weary in doing good, for in due season we shall reap, if we do not give up." (Galatians 6:9 NIV). However, grit alone isn't sustainable. Even the strongest minds eventually tire. That's why God, in His mercy, adds **grace.**

The Power of Grace

Grace is not permission to quit; it's power to continue. "My grace is sufficient for you, for My power is made perfect in weakness." (2 Corinthians 12:9 NIV). Grace is divine assistance. It's God stepping in where your effort runs out. It's the quiet strength that lifts your head, renews your heart, and fills your lungs with courage once more. When grit says, "I can't go on," grace says, "I'll carry you."

Grit + Grace = Endurance

Grit and grace are partners, not opposites. You don't have to choose between working hard and trusting God; you can do both.

- **Grit** keeps you committed.
- **Grace** keeps you connected.

God never asked you to be strong without Him. He invites you to bring your work into His presence and let grace multiply your efforts.

Signs You Need Fresh Grace

1. **You're grinding but not growing.**
2. **You feel spiritually dry, even while serving.**
3. **You're performing rather than partnering with God.**
4. **You feel irritable, numb, or resentful of your calling.**

These are not signs of failure, they're signals. And grace is the remedy.

How to Access Fresh Grace

1. Return to the Secret Place
Grace flows from intimacy. Stop everything else and go back to prayer, not performance prayer but raw, honest, unfiltered conversation with God.

2. Rest Without Shame
Sabbath is sacred. You are not less spiritual for taking a break; you are obedient. Rest is a weapon when it's surrendered to God.

3. Repent from Self-Reliance

When you try to "grit" your way through without God, burnout is inevitable. Invite Him back into every detail, even the boring ones.

4. Receive Daily Manna

Grace doesn't always come in giant waves. Often, it comes in daily doses: a Scripture, a song, a friend's voice, a whisper from the Holy Spirit. "Give us this day our daily bread…" (Matthew 6:11 NIV). You don't need enough grace for next year, just for today.

Leadership Insight: Leading from the overflow

As a leader, you need not just grit but also overflow. People can feel when you're ministering on fumes. Your strength may inspire them, but your dependence on grace will transform them. Your team, your family, and your church don't need a superhero; they need someone surrendered, someone who knows how to rest in grace and keep going.

A Final Word to the Weary Warrior

Maybe you've been grinding in silence. Maybe you're tired of being strong for everyone else. Maybe you're at the end of your rope. Here's the truth: God gives more grace (James 4:6 NIV). Not because you earned it, but because He is with you, for you, and in you. Don't let grit become a god; let grace be your gear. You were never meant to carry this alone. You're not just surviving; you're being sustained. You're still standing because of **grace for the grit.**

Journal notes

Chapter 8
The Silence Between Seasons

There are moments in the journey when the voice of God seems quiet. No new instructions. No open doors. Just stillness. Silence. Waiting. These are not wasted seasons; they are sacred pauses, the silence between one season ending and another beginning. A divine interlude where God does His deepest work not around you, but within you.

When Heaven Goes Quiet

Have you ever prayed with urgency and heard nothing back? Have you looked for signs and found none? Have you waited for movement, but everything remained still? Welcome to the silence between seasons. Even Jesus experienced it. "He was led by the Spirit into the wilderness..." (Luke 4:1 NIV). Heaven was silent. Yet Jesus was still in the centre of God's will. Silence is not absence. Delay is not denial. Stillness is not stagnation.

Why God Allows Silence

1. To Test Our Trust
When you can't trace God, will you still trust Him? Silence tests if our faith is built on results or relationship.

2. To Strengthen Our Sensitivity
Silence sharpens our ears. When the loud stops, the subtle becomes sacred. We start to hear God in whispers, Scripture, creation, and stillness.

3. To Prepare Us for the Next Assignment
The space between seasons is often where identity is refined and vision is clarified. It's where we learn obedience, humility, and endurance.

Biblical Example: Elijah in the cave

Elijah expected God to appear in wind, fire, and earthquake. However, God came in a gentle whisper (1 Kings 19:11-12 NIV), not in drama, but in stillness.

How to Steward the Silence

1. Remain in Position

Keep doing what He last told you to do. Don't move just because you're uncomfortable. Obedience isn't seasonal. "Be still, and know that I am God..." (Psalm 46:10 NIV).

2. Feed Your Faith, Not Your Fear

The enemy also loves to speak in the silence, sowing doubt and discouragement. Combat his lies with truth. Meditate on Scripture. Speak life. Guard your thoughts.

3. Record the Revelations

Silence often births subtle insight. Keep a journal. Write down what God reveals in dreams, impressions, and Scripture. When the next season begins, those notes will guide you.

4. Don't Manufacture Movement

Avoid the temptation to *force* something new. Ishmael was born when Abraham and Sarah grew tired of waiting for God's promise. Don't create counterfeit blessings out of impatience.

Leadership Insight: The power of quiet leadership

Leaders often feel pressure to always have a word, a plan, or a next step. However, true leadership involves exercising restraint. There's power in saying, "God hasn't spoken yet, so we're staying still." Your silence, if spirit-led, can be more powerful than a thousand strategies. Your people don't just need your voice; they need your **discernment**.

Encouragement for the In-between

If you're in a season where nothing seems to be moving, don't quit. This is your *cave moment*. Your *wilderness chapter*. Your *preparation season*. God is not punishing you. He's positioning you. The silence is not void; it's **pregnant with purpose**.

And when God speaks again, it will be with clarity, direction, and momentum. Until then:

- Wait well.
- Worship anyway.
- Keep walking faithfully.

"Though it lingers, wait for it; it will certainly come and will not delay." (Habakkuk 2:3 NIV). You are not lost. You are not forgotten. You are simply between seasons. Hold on.

Journal notes

Chapter 9
When the Finish Line Moves

What happens when what you were running toward... moves? You trained. You prayed. You pushed. You mapped it out. You set goals. You saw the destination in sight, and just when you were about to reach it, life shifted. The goalpost moved. The job changed. The person left. The outcome flipped. This chapter is for those who kept running only to discover the finish line wasn't where they thought it would be.

The Reality of Shifting Seasons

Sometimes God allows our "finish lines" to move, not to punish us, but to mature us. Just as a shepherd redirects a sheep when danger or a better pasture lies ahead, God reroutes us for our own good. "In their hearts humans plan their course, but the Lord establishes their steps." (Proverbs 16:9 NIV). Your plans were good, but His are better. It doesn't mean you failed; it means the journey is still unfolding.

The Disappointment of Delay

Let's be real: when the goal shifts, it can feel like betrayal. You feel:

- **Confused:** "Why did I sense peace before?"
- **Frustrated:** "I was *so* close!"
- **Embarrassed:** "People were watching me."
- **Exhausted:** "I don't know if I can keep going."

This is where many are tempted to quit, not because they lack faith, but because they did not expect the road to change.

But God says:
"Behold, I am doing a new thing! Now it springs up; do you not perceive it?" (Isaiah 43:19 NIV). God isn't moving you away from your purpose when the finish line moves. He's moving you **into** it.

Biblical Example: Joseph's detour

Joseph dreamed of leadership. But instead of a palace, he found himself in a pit... then a prison. Each time, the finish line moved. Yet every step was part of the process.

When Joseph finally stepped into his destiny, he realized: "You meant it for evil, but God meant it for good." (Genesis 50:20 NIV). The detour was divine.

Leadership Insight: Adjusting without abandoning

As a leader, shifting goals doesn't mean shifting loyalty. Hold tightly to your *why* but loosely to the *how*.

- **Don't panic, pivot.**
- **Don't abandon, adapt.**
- **Don't freeze, reframe.**

You're still leading; you're simply navigating an evolving landscape. People will follow a leader who can admit, "I didn't expect this, but we're going to grow through it."

What to Do When the Finish Line Moves

1. Reevaluate Your Vision
Was your vision from God or yourself? A vision given by God can be tested, stretched, and delayed, but it never dies.

2. Release Control

You're not a failure because the plan changed. You're faithful because you persevered through the change. Let go of your need to know everything. Clarity often comes after obedience.

3. Run at God's Pace
Some finish lines are delayed because you must walk with God, not sprint without Him. Trust His timing; He knows when you're ready.

4. Celebrate Your Progress
Even if the line moves, look at how far you've come. Don't let a shifting goal erase your growth. Every step you've taken has built character, strength, and wisdom.

You're Still in the Race

Just because the goal has moved doesn't mean you've lost. It means God has more in store. You're not running in circles; you're running through layers of purpose. Each delay and every shift is a divine recalibration. So, tie your laces tighter. Square your shoulders again. Look up. The finish line hasn't disappeared; it has just changed shape. "Blessed is the one who perseveres under trial because, having stood the test, that person will receive the crown of life..." (James 1:12 NIV)

Journal notes

Chapter 10
Quitting is Not an Option

Every step you've taken. Every tear you've shed. Every chapter in this journey... has led you here: **The decision to keep going.** You've faced discouragement, delay, betrayal, fear, silence, and uncertainty. You've stood at the edge of giving up more times than you can count. And yet, something deeper inside you has refused to stop. That something is **calling**. That someone is **God**. This final chapter is not just a conclusion; it's a *commission*. You are being sent back into the fight, but with fire in your bones, steel in your spine, and vision in your eyes.

What Does it Really Mean Never to Quit?

"Not quitting" doesn't mean you never feel tired. It doesn't mean you never question the path. It means that no matter what comes, you **stand**, **lean on God**, and **show up anyway**. "Having done all... to stand."

(Ephesians 6:13 NIV). There is holy dignity in not quitting.

The Battle Within

Let's be honest, most quitting doesn't happen externally. It happens **internally**:

- You give up in your heart, but keep going in habit.
- You show up to the job, the pulpit, the family dinner, but inside, you've already surrendered.

This is your call to reclaim the fight **from within.** You are not a quitter; you are a **contender.**

Biblical Encouragement for the Final Push

1. **Jesus in Gethsemane:** Even Jesus wrestled with the desire to let the cup pass from Him. But He stayed. He obeyed. He overcame. (Luke 22:42 NIV)
2. **Paul the Apostle:** Shipwrecked, imprisoned, and beaten, but still preaching. "I have fought the good fight... I have kept the faith." (2 Timothy 4:7 NIV)
3. **Job:** Lost everything, yet he declared, "Though He slay me, yet will I trust Him." (Job 13:15 NIV).

These weren't superhumans. They were **submitted humans**. That's the difference.

What Finishing Looks Like

- It doesn't always look like applause.
- It might not come with a promotion.
- Crowds may not recognise it.

Finishing well means staying faithful until God says it's done. "Well done, good and faithful servant…" (Matthew 25:23 NIV). That's the finish line worth chasing.

Legacy Over Longevity

Sometimes, we fear quitting because we must keep doing what we've always done. But staying in the race doesn't always mean staying in the *same role*.

- Elijah passed the mantle to Elisha.
- Paul handed the churches to Timothy and Titus.
- Jesus empowered the disciples and ascended.

Quitting is not about **retiring** from responsibility but about **repositioning** yourself purposefully. You don't quit the call. You evolve in how you walk it out.

For the Reader Who's Ready to Give Up

If this book finds you at your breaking point, this is your moment of mercy. God's not mad at you. He's not disappointed. But He's not done with you either. If you're out of strength, He will carry you. If you're out of vision, He will speak again. He will breathe life into your bones if you're out of courage. You have been chosen, anointed, and preserved **for this exact moment**. Not just to survive it, but to rise through it.

Declare This Over Your Life:

I am not a quitter.
I am not my failures.
I am not the voice of fear.
I am a finisher.
I am called.
I am covered.
I am committed.
And by the grace of God, I will not give up.

Journal notes

Final Word from Dr. R. van Reenen

Dear reader,

I wrote this book not because I've never wanted to quit, but because I've faced that temptation head-on. I know what it's like to weep in private while leading in public. I understand the ache of unseen sacrifice and the weight of unfulfilled dreams. But I also recognise the **power of endurance**. God is not looking for perfection. He's looking for perseverance. He's not looking for heroes. He's looking for hearts that stay soft and hands that stay open.

The call on your life is too precious to forfeit. The people assigned to your voice are too valuable to abandon. The God who called you is too faithful to disappoint. So, if you remember nothing else from this book, remember this:

Quitting is not an option.

You were born for this. Now, finish what He started in you. With fire and faith.

Dr. R. van Reenen

Appendix: Tools for the Journey

This appendix is designed to be your **toolkit,** filled with Scripture, reflection questions, action steps, and declarations to help you **keep going** when the temptation to quit resurfaces. Whether you're a leader, a student, a parent, a pastor, or simply someone navigating life, you'll find strength here.

A. Key Scriptures for Endurance

These verses are anchors for moments of weakness:

1. Isaiah 40:31
"But those who hope in the Lord will renew their strength. They will soar on wings like eagles…"

2. Galatians 6:9
"Let us not become weary in doing good, for at the proper time we will reap a harvest if we do not give up."

3. 2 Corinthians 4:8-9
"We are hard pressed on every side, but not crushed; perplexed, but not in despair…"

4. James 1:12
"Blessed is the one who perseveres under trial…"

5. Philippians 1:6

"He who began a good work in you will carry it on to completion..."

B. Personal Reflection Questions

Take time to reflect and journal your answers:

1. What are the moments in my life when I've wanted to give up?
2. What helped me keep going during those times?
3. What patterns do I notice when I feel overwhelmed?
4. Who are the people God has placed around me for support?
5. What is one dream I know I must not quit on?

C. Ten Daily Declarations

Speak these out loud every morning:

1. I am stronger than I feel.
2. I am called for a purpose.
3. I will not quit when things get tough.
4. I walk by faith, not by sight.
5. I am not defined by failure.
6. I have heaven's help and backing.
7. I am surrounded by grace.
8. I am growing through this process.
9. I have what I need to finish well.
10. Today, I choose to keep going.

D. Action Steps When You Feel Like Quitting

1. Pause and Breathe
Take a 15-minute break, get fresh air, or sit in silence. Recentre.

2. Phone a Friend
Call someone who lifts your spirit, don't isolate.

3. Write a Letter to God
Pour out your heart in a raw, unfiltered prayer.

4. Remind Yourself of Your "Why"
Revisit your vision, journal entries, or the first moment you said "yes."

5. Worship Loudly
Music realigns the soul. Praise shifts the atmosphere.

E. For Leaders: How to encourage others not to quit

- Share your own battles. People follow authenticity.
- Preach perseverance, not just prosperity.
- Acknowledge pain without idolizing it.
- Equip people with tools, not just motivation.
- Keep showing up, it permits others to do the same.

F. Final Encouragement

You may revisit this book multiple times in your life. That's okay. Every time you face a new battle; the words may take on deeper meaning. Keep this appendix as your **spiritual first aid kit,** a reminder that you have resources to fight back when the fire gets hot and the pressure feels unbearable. Let the Holy Spirit be your coach, the Scriptures be your sword, and your testimony be your weapon. The journey isn't easy, but it is worth it. You're not alone. You're not weak. You're not done. You are called. You are chosen. You are a finisher.

About the Author

Dr. R. Van Reenen is a distinguished humanitarian, theologian, life coach, and business advisor to prominent mining houses across the African continent. Born in Cape Town, South Africa, he is the eldest son of Bishop Walter James and Maureen Van Reenen and the oldest of five siblings. From humble beginnings and a life marked by poverty, Dr. Van Reenen has journeyed through adversity with unwavering vision and determined focus on his goals.

With a deep conviction to spiritually and economically empower lives, Dr. Van Reenen holds an MBA and a Ph.D. in Religion and Economics. He founded the School of Spiritual Economics, where biblical principles and practical financial wisdom intersect. He also serves as the chairman of Dr. R. Van Reenen Ministries International, a global ministry dedicated to restoring purpose, igniting faith, and advancing the Kingdom of God. In addition, he founded KBFI (Kingdom Bishops Fraternal International)—a spiritual alliance that unites apostolic and episcopal leaders across denominations.

Dr. Van Reenen's calling is rooted in his belief that every life has a divine purpose and that pain often serves as a pathway to power. His message embodies perseverance, vision, and faith that refuses to surrender.

Faith Statement:
"I believe that God calls us not only to endure, but to overcome, and to do so with purpose. Every challenge is an invitation to trust Him more deeply. We do not quit because the One who called us is faithful."

Scripture Reference:
"Being confident of this very thing, that He who has begun a good work in you will complete it until the day of Jesus Christ."
Philippians 1:6 (NKJV)

Dr. R Van Reenen Ministries
Email: info@drvanreenenministries.co.za
Website: www.drvanreenenministries.co.za

Acknowledgements

First, I thank the Lord Jesus Christ, my sustainer, my hope, and my unfailing source of wisdom. Every page of this book is a testament to Your strength working through my weakness.

To my family, thank you for your patience during early mornings, late nights, and all the moments in between. Your love has made this possible.

To the leaders, pastors, mentors, and friends who have walked beside me, you are living proof that iron sharpens iron. Your encouragement kept me going when the road grew dim. To every reader holding this book, I see you. I wrote this for you. Your journey matters, your pain is valid, and your perseverance is powerful.

And to everyone who said I couldn't or wouldn't, thank you. You reminded me that *quitting is not an option.*

With gratitude,
Dr. R. van Reenen

For Book Sales and Purchases:

Now available for purchase on Takealot, Amazon, and selected bookstores.

Guest Speaking and Bookings:

Readers and event organizers may use the website and email contact provided for any guest speaking engagements, interviews, or ministry invitations.

info@drvanreenenministries.co.za
www.drvanreenenministries.co.za

***